STOP
FOR SOLITUDE

THE POWER OF ASSESSING YOUR YEAR BEFORE PROCEEDING TO THE NEW

Hello Friend,

Thanks so much for purchasing this workbook. God really impressed on my heart to put this workbook together.

I have been a personal growth and development coach and mentor for over 2 decades with a passion to teach, train and facilitate transformation for Gods children so they can develop and deploy their God given potentials and live a maximised life.

The contents of this workbook have been tried and tested by many, myself included for many years and I have fruits to show that this questions if honestly and truthfully answered can significantly change the trajectory of your new year and give you many desired results.

I personally commit quality time to setting myself aside and answering those questions, allowing the Holy Spirit to really flash His truth where it is needed, because I always mostly achieve my yearly set out goals, I look forward to rewarding myself after the assessment and setting myself new challenge for the new year just to continue to increase my capacity.

For those who have never had a spiritual midwife to help you start your development journey I have a resourced website where you can visit and take some of my courses@ restartyou.ruthmateola.com

If you will like a one of session for me to help you look at your answers and give you a well guided approach to maximise your new year email me at ruth@ruthmateola.com, note there is a charge for this session.

In 2024 I will be facilitating and hosting a few events that will help you on this journey.

For more information about any of this event please email- ruth@ruthmateola.com

I will also love to hear your feedback on how this workbook has helped you and if I should create more like it.

Be blessed.

Pastor Ruth Mateola

We 've all had 365 days that God has blessed us with in 2023 and as we prepare to round up this calendar year, I am a firm believer of honest self-assessment.

One of the biggest lies you can believe is that you do not need to change, that everything about you is ok the way it is. It is the most destructive pattern of thinking anyone can accept.

Unfortunately, I have seen many Christians embrace this deadly believe and because they're gifted and anointed, they do not pursue change.

Every new year is a new opportunity to pursue change, no matter how gifted, blessed, or spiritual you are there will always be room for better to become best.

Nuggets –

- The first step in crafting the life you want is to get rid of everything you don't."

- You can't reach for anything new if your hands are still full of yesterday's junk.

- Clutter is the physical manifestation of unmade decisions fuelled by procrastination.

Luke 14:28-29 - For which of you, intending to build a tower, does not sit down first and count the cost, whether he has *enough* to finish *it*— 29 lest, after he has laid the foundation, and is not able to finish, all who see *it* begin to mock him, 30 saying, 'This man began to build and was not able to finish'?

Ephesians 4: 22- 24 - To put off your old self, which belongs to your former manner of life and is corrupt through deceitful desires, and to be renewed in the spirit of your minds, and to put on the new self, created after the likeness of God in true righteousness and holiness.

Every new year requires new mind, strategies, structures, goals, and dedication, if you do not do a good job assessing your previous year you run the risk of repeating the same things the same ways that does not yield your desired results.

Self-assessment must be taken and done on a very serious level, it requires a good investment of time and space that is conducive to really assess your entire year in the right way that will give you a good enough picture for you to use to map out a new year that will be productive and fruitful.

I want to encourage a time of solitude; I have used this so many times and it's the best way to get a thorough assessment done.

Retreat is about a time of solitude and it's an effective way of separating yourself from the noise to assess your life , when you retreat to assess it give you the opportunity to understanding what is wrong, how did it go wrong, how does it make you feel now, making a decision that you are no longer ok with stagnation, pain, lack of fulfilment, dormant potentials, gifts and abilities, you need to heal from the pain, disappointment, betrayal, loss whatever it is that caused you to think you need to stop and restart.

Many times the enemy convinces us we do not have the time to take away and get to a quiet place of thinking and understanding, and because we do not prioritise assessment we keep going in a vicious cycle of doing the same thing expecting a different results, but if you are going to be gifted another 365 days by God you better prioritise a time away for self-assessment, which by the way God extends into not just discovering the things you are doing wrong or done wrong but He begins to give you a picture of what he wants you to pursue in the new year.

Mark 6:31 - And he said to them, "Come away by yourselves to a desolate place and rest a while." For many were coming and going, and they had no leisure even to eat.

From the above scripture its quite evidence that even Jesus our prototype took the issue of retreat very seriously, as powerful and anointed as he was getting away to a quiet place for assessment and realignment was important. being a pastor and a mentor, I see that many of us struggle with snatching ourselves away from the busyness of life to actually take the time to go be with the Lord and not just assess but be refreshed and redirected.

I cannot over emphasise, we plan holidays, vacations, SPA days, parties etc but we never plan to go and be alone by ourself and with God, we carry issues, problems, anxieties, worry, frustration all through the year because we don't retreat, my biggest encouragement for you is this issue of RETREAT, please don't just do it because you are assessing how this year has gone for you, plan a few into your calendar in the new year.

Retreats offer the benefit of physical, emotional, and psychological withdrawal from the stresses and strains of everyday life: a chance to escape from the toxic effects of noise, information overload, unrealistic demands, and the frantic busy-ness of 21s century living; to enjoy a safe haven in which to start to recover from trauma and to heal on all levels.

A Retreat can be a wonderful experience, a booster, and an accelerator. Much can be realized in a short time in shifting perception and re-establishing what really matters. However, the benefits achieved will be lost unless you act on your return in respect of self-care to avoid a return to overwhelm and stress overload.

Retreats remove us from noise and distraction, and into a place of spiritual refreshing and renewing. It is a way of entering into the presence of God and allowing him to nourish our soul. As we settle into the stillness, we notice the stirrings of our soul, our deeper longings, and God's quiet whisper to us.

Benefits of retreat

- **Wonderfully rewarding on many levels**

  A Retreat can be a life-changing experience providing true 'me time' to reconnect with your authentic self, to remember what brings you joy, and to achieve the clarity to start creating the means to have it.

- **Refreshing, rejuvenating, re-energising and re-empowering**

  So often we are at the limit of our endurance when we take a break (and for many a holiday with 'loved ones' is far from a relaxing experience). A retreat can recharge batteries on many levels and bring new insights for positive life change.

- **Deep relaxation and peace**
  of mind bringing physical, mental and emotional benefits and also disconnecting you from all the demands, pressures, etc back home that pull you in so many directions. It is impossible to put a price on the profound benefit of being helped to connect with inner stillness and to find solace. The solitude of a retreat can provides a pause in the constant, unremitting demands of daily life. Time to reflect, renew and restore. Relaxing the mind is the natural complement to relaxing the body and to dealing with 21st century stressors.

- **Sacred space and spiritual connection**

  When you experience the profound inner connection with the Divine within yourself, all of life makes much more sense, and is much more fun!

- **Disconnect from Technology and Reconnect with Yourself**

  One of the biggest benefits of going on a retreat is the opportunity to disconnect from technology and reconnect with yourself. In our modern world, we are constantly bombarded with notifications, emails, and social media updates, which can leave us feeling stressed and overwhelmed. By taking a break from technology, you can give your mind a chance to rest and recharge.

This can help you feel more present, focused, and mindful, which can have a positive impact on your overall well-being.

- **Gain Clarity and Perspective on Your Life**

  Going on a retreat can provide you with the space and time you need to reflect on your life and gain clarity and perspective. When you are caught up in the day-to-day routine, it can be difficult to see the bigger picture and make important decisions. By stepping away from your usual environment and routine, you can gain fresh perspective on your life and priorities. This can help you make infirmed decisions and set goal that align with your values and aspirations.

- **Return Home Refreshed and Energised**

  One of the biggest benefits of going on a retreat is the opportunity to return home feeling refreshed and energized. By taking a break from your daily routine and responsibilities, you can recharge your batteries and come back with a renewed sense of purpose and motivation. This can help you tackle challenges with a fresh perspective and approach tasks with more enthusiasm. Additionally, the relaxation and self-care practices you engage in during a retreat can help reduce stress and improve your overall well-being, leading to increased energy and vitality.

Before we proceed let's discover a few things.

What is self-assessment?

Self-assessment is the process of looking at oneself in order to assess aspects that are important to one's identity. It is one of the motives that drive self – evaluation along with – verification and self – enhancement. It helps to evaluate oneself of our actions, attitudes and performance.

Self-assessment helps in understanding your core qualities and finding out your capacity and progress. Self-assessment determines your responsibility and engagement. It shapes what support you need to build and brings a hones awareness for a honest decision on what you need to change. It is never a negative exercise, and it should never be viewed as such, if you view it negatively it simply means you are unwilling to discover your own truth and intentionally make the necessary changes.

Simply put, self-evaluation is the ability to examine yourself to find out how much progress you have made. It requires employees to monitor their own abilities and evaluate strengths and weaknesses. It puts employees largely in charge of their own development.

A self-evaluation means considering questions such as:

- Where have you excelled?
- What achievements are you most proud of?
- Where do you feel you need more support?
- What goals do you wish you could have accomplished?
- What would help you to accomplish these goals?
- What do you most like about your job?
- What do you most dislike about your job?
- What improvements could be made to make your role easier?
- What components of your job would you like to eliminate and why?
- What career goals to you hope to accomplish in the next three years?

These are the kind of questions included in a self-evaluation – ones that prompt thought about performance. The purpose of a self-assessment is to help an individual know the extent of their abilities and to improve upon them. It can be daunting to when you do this for the first time, but over time it will become more natural.

At the end of year, I ask myself 4 pertinent questions which forms my self-assessment session, please feel free to include others that you feel is necessary to give you the right picture you need. I have to tell you over the last decade of my life and ministry doing this yearly ritual has been a tremendous help to me. I take the retreat time seriously and I take answering the questions honestly has been a life saver.

- **What worked and why?**
- **What did not work and why?**
- **What must I change in me for it to work next year?**
- **What new thing must I learn to enhance my growth in the New Year?**

Romans 12:3 - For by the grace given to me I say to everyone among you not to think of himself more highly than he ought to think, but to think with sober judgment, each according to the measure of faith that God has assigned.

2 Corinthians 13:5 -Examine yourselves, to see whether you are in the faith. Test yourselves. Or do you not realize this about yourselves, that Jesus Christ is in you? —unless indeed you fail to meet the test!

Proverbs 14:8 - The wisdom of the prudent is to discern his way, but the folly of fools is deceiving.

I feel one of the greatest testimonies to our life is that we are constantly changing and being more like Christ and moving more into the plan of God for our lives. When you assess yourself there must be a strong desire in you to see opportunity for change and to deliberately pursue it. So here we go.

1) **Write out what this year has been for you. What did God tell you about this year? What were your key instructions? What was your vision for the year? Please be honest yet objective. What clear picture did you go into 2023 with that informed your goals? What resources did you go into the year with? What were those key pressure areas you went in wanting to change?**

) **What worked for you this year and why? If any. I am talking in terms of goals you set for yourself and what happened with them.**

3) **What did not work for you this year and why? Please make no excuse just tell it as it is**.

4) **List those challenges / sabotages that hindered you to not allow things to work this year and please know as a mentor I know a few.**

) Lessons learned are "the knowledge gained during a project, which shows how project were addressed or should be addressed in the future, for the purpose of improving future performance." Every goal we set is a project that must be delivered, but we understand that things may go according to plan or not. List me those things you learnt this year that you will not have to go through again in the coming New Year.

6) **Stagnation is a silent killer, and it is introduced in our life by a spirit calle** complacency. Complacency never encourages or demands change fror

you, it tells you a lie that you are ok the way you are and there is no need for change. Any life that will experience success and progress must see and embrace change as an opportunity and not an inconvenience. You are where you are right now because of the changes you were willing or not willing to change. So, list here -What must I change in me for it to work next year?

7) Every new year must include new learning and information, the reason why we are not smashing our goals or getting to our desired or pursued destination could be because we are trying to put new wine in an old wineskin, we want to keep using the same dull axe to chip away new path and from personal experience that does not work. What new thing must I learn to enhance my growth in the New Year?

One of the hold ups of goal achievement, please not there are many but that is no covered in this volume, one main one is CAPACITY.

Capacity is defined as an individual's mental or physical ability. Matthew 25 talks abou the parable of the talent, everyone excels according to how they use their ability capacity to push themselves. When we talk about capacity we also look at the structure o your life in the year and the routines you set up that enhanced your capacity. How hav you increased your capacity in the following areas this year? The honest answers wi show you the pit holes and help you plan and execute better in the new year.

Spiritually:

Physically:

Emotionally:

Financially:

Leadership, if you have been given opportunity to lead anything:

3) What other capacity did you build on this year? E.g. networking, helping other ministries etc.

9) **What has been your predominant view/ attitude this year and how has it helped or affected you. I want you to look deep and analyse here the pattern of thinking that fuelled those attitudes and articulate the fruits of those attitudes both positive and negative.**

10) What were your untapped, unused resources, convictions and gifts, and divine instructions, this is so key because if it is not changed the cycle will repeat itself.

11) Who was guiding you this year in your development? How did you take that relationship? What are your fruits of that relationship?

12) After all you have answered above, now do a SWOT Analysis on yourself as you project into a new year. What is your SWOT Analysis? Its your

Strength

Weaknesses

Opportunities

Threats

13) Capture 2023 overall.

14) Now that you have taken this much needed solitude time and you have answered the above questions by now, I know the Holy Spirit has already started to speak to you about the new year approaching. Every new year must have some elements in this that will under guard you to maximising it.

- Clarity of vision
- Plan
- Resources
- Strategy
- Accountability
- Expected fruits.

Use the rest of this workbook to begin to put down your holy spirit revelations and instructions about the new year using the above parameters. Please note you are not limited to them thy are simply guidelines, be completely free to write it down and make it plain as the spirit leads so that you can run with it.

15) Any other thoughts?

STOP

FOR SOLITUDE

THE POWER OF ASSESSING YOUR YEAR BEFORE PROCEEDING TO THE NEW

Printed in Great Britain
by Amazon

34689688R00015